Play Together

INSPIRED BY
Randi Mahomes
AND Teresa Jane

WRITTEN AND ILLUSTRATED BY
Lenora Riegel

Copyright 2024 by Siphre Books siphrebooks.com. All rights reserved.
ISBN 978-1-952765-15-5

Collaboration: Randi Mahomes and Teresa Jane
Author and Illustrator: Lenora Riegel
Art Director: Katie Honas
Copy Editor: Elizabeth Shay
Co-editor: Sharon (SOS) Riegel

Published by Siphre Books
All rights reserved. No part of this book can be reproduced in any form by any electronic or mechanical means, including storage and retrieval systems, without written permission from the publisher, except for reviewers who may quote passages in a review.
1098765432
First Edition

RANDI MAHOMES was raised in a small East Texas town where everyone knew everyone and friendships last forever. She is very close with her school-yard friends, many of whom she met during her faith journey to church. Randi and one of her besties, **TERESA JANE**, met at the age of eleven at a joined church summer skating outing and the rest is history. They share a strong belief in kindness and giving the glory to God while navigating a world that's not always easy or nice—but with friends, it's easier.

I love you with a love that will last forever. JEREMIAH 31:3

Miss Martha's students are learning to play together. She turned to her 3rd grade class "Playtime!" she said. "Let's go outside!"

Jumping up from her desk, Mary bumped Ruth. "Sorry I bumped you," said Mary.

"It's ok to make mistakes. Everyone does," said Miss Martha.

"I apologize for my mistakes."
FORGIVE EACH OTHER. MICAH 7:18

Joseph spotted a boy sitting on the bench. Saying hello and feeling no fear, Joseph said, "Hi! Is this your first day?"

"Yes. Hi, I'm Lucas."

Miss Martha smiled. "I'm pleased to see all the students playing together. Everyone is accepted on the playground.

"I am welcoming, and I respect my friends' differences."

ACCEPT EACH OTHER. ROMANS 15:7

Ruth and Isaac worked together to arrange the ball rack.
"Can you use an extra hand?" asked Simon.

"I work hard. I'm happy to help."
DO YOUR BEST. ECCLESIASTES 9:10

"I'm getting better and better," said Ethan, bouncing the ball to square number two.

"Yes! You're improving and following directions," said Miss Martha. "Your leadership makes me smile."

"I ask a question if I don't understand, so I keep learning more. I keep trying."

I HAVE NOT YET REACHED MY GOAL. BUT, I CONTINUE TO TRY. COLOSSIANS 3:23

Issac saw Tarah looking worried and asked her why.
"Thank you for listening to my worries," Tarah said.

"I listen when someone needs to talk about their feelings."

COMFORT EACH OTHER AND GIVE EACH OTHER STRENGTH. THESSALONIANS 5:11

Miss Martha heard cheering from the students by the slide.

"You did it!"

"Way to go!"

"Hurray, Hope! You went down the slide for your first time!"

"I am not afraid to try new things."

BE STRONG AND BRAVE.
DEUTERONOMY 31:6

"Simon, you dropped your bracelet."

"Oh! Thanks, Julia. That was a gift from my dad."

"I am kind to my friends and family."
BE KIND TO ONE ANOTHER. EPHESIANS 4:32

Mary noticed Esther crying.

"What's wrong?" asked Mary.

"I lost my pet toad, Warty," sniffed Esther. "He leaped out of my hand and hopped away!"

"Oh no! You must be so sad," said Mary. "I'm here if you need me."

"I smile to show I care."

BE SAD WITH THOSE WHO ARE SAD.
PSALM 34:18

Miss Martha grinned when the students shared the ball, took turns, and then waited for their turn to play.

"You've got this, Julia," Hope cheered.

"I am grateful for my friends' help. I say please and thank you using my manners."

DO GOOD TO OTHERS. HEBREWS 13:16

"This is my fifth time trying this climb," said Lucas.

"I've got you," said Caleb. "Grab hold of my hand."

"I never give up and encourage my friends to keep trying."

NEVER GIVE UP. PHILIPPIANS 4:13

"I need to tell you something," said Esther. "My tummy hurts."

Miss Martha listened, thought about her words before responding, and watched Ester's reaction.

"I pay attention when talking."

WHEN YOU TALK, ALWAYS BE KIND AND WISE.
COLOSSIANS 4:6

"I like playing inside and reading books," Rufus said.

"Not me!" answered Caleb "I like to play outside!"

"I can disagree and still like my friends."

TRY TO LIVE IN PEACE WITH ALL PEOPLE.
HEBREWS 12:14

"I love eating dandelions," said Lucas.

"Dandelions never give up," said Mary. "They come back, even when they get picked."

"Let's not eat off the ground," Miss Martha said. "Promise me you'll only eat from your snack bag."

Mary, Tarah, and Lucas said, "We promise."

"I keep my promises."
KEEP PROMISES. ROMANS 4:21

"Recess is over!" Miss Martha called. "We'll have more fun together tomorrow!"

"Everyone is welcome on the playground."

"Play together!"

ACCEPT EACH OTHER. ROMANS 15:7